Purronnas Tales Publishing

ISBN: 146371193X
ISBN-13: 9781463711931

There are many individuals who motivated me to write this book, but I will name only a few. Ms. Glass gave me the seed, and my art teachers nourished my courage by believing in me. Mom was there when I needed her and was understanding when I took time alone to write. Dad always had faith in my art; I miss him a lot and wish he would give me a sign. Larry, my relentless brother, provided valuable input. Grandpa Leo rescued many homeless or abused animals. Aunt Annie passed her love of animals to me and added many stepping stones in my path of life. My dear college friend Susan offered her help when I needed it most, and I thank her for her expertise.

Last, but not least, I thank all the animals that have touched my heart. This book is dedicated to them. Tami, my precious first dog, taught me much about respect and love. Thus began my love for animals and their welfare. We must speak up for animals because they cannot speak for themselves, and we must protect them from people who neglect and abuse them. My cats and foster dogs have helped me through the most arduous and frightening time in my life, and I love them forever.

This book is about bullying and how being aware of our differences can enrich our lives. I hope this book will help children and animals in some way. My beloved tabby cat waddles over me as I write. This book is a labor of love, and I hope you will enjoy it. ♥

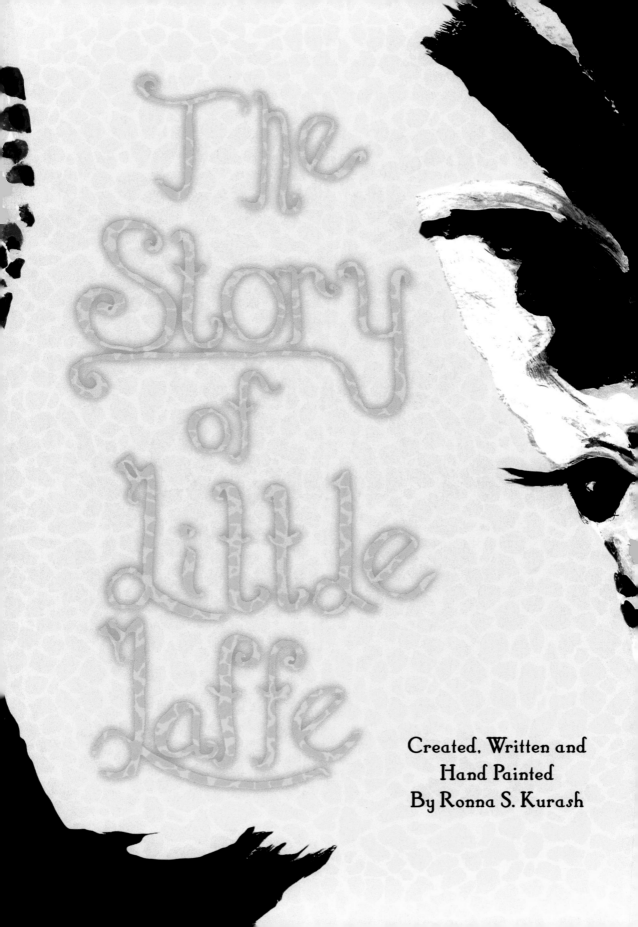

The Story of Little Jaffe

Created, Written and
Hand Painted
By Ronna S. Kurash

Many years ago,

long before Marilyn Monroe,

in The Tropical
Forest of
Perfect,

there lived a non-perfect giraffe.

Her eyes, ears and nose
were like those of her mother,
but her neck was unlike any other.

The neck was their most
important feature,
for a long, sleek neck
made them unique
from any other creature.

The small-necked giraffe would
cry all day
while the other giraffes would
play and say:

"You are such a small
and strange giraffe

that we will call you
'Little Laffe!'"

Little Laffe would cry
for days on end
because the other
giraffes would not be her friend.

She continued to cry
and cry for days

as the other giraffes snubbed her
in many ways.

When nighttime approached
she would be by herself,

and she was afraid
that she might need help.

While the other giraffes munched
on leaves that grew high,

Little Laffe would sit
nearby and sigh.

She was, after all, far too small
to reach the trees that grew so tall.

She would patiently
wait for the rest to be done

to eat crumbled leftovers
dried by the sun.

As time passed on,

feeling timid and very hurt,
she found the spunk to loudly
blurt:

"You are close-minded and
should change your cruel way.

I am tired of you calling me
whatever you may!

You are mean to me
and you bully me so.
You think you are smart
but what do you know?

I may look different
because my neck is small,
but you are not kind and are nasty
and have plenty of gall!

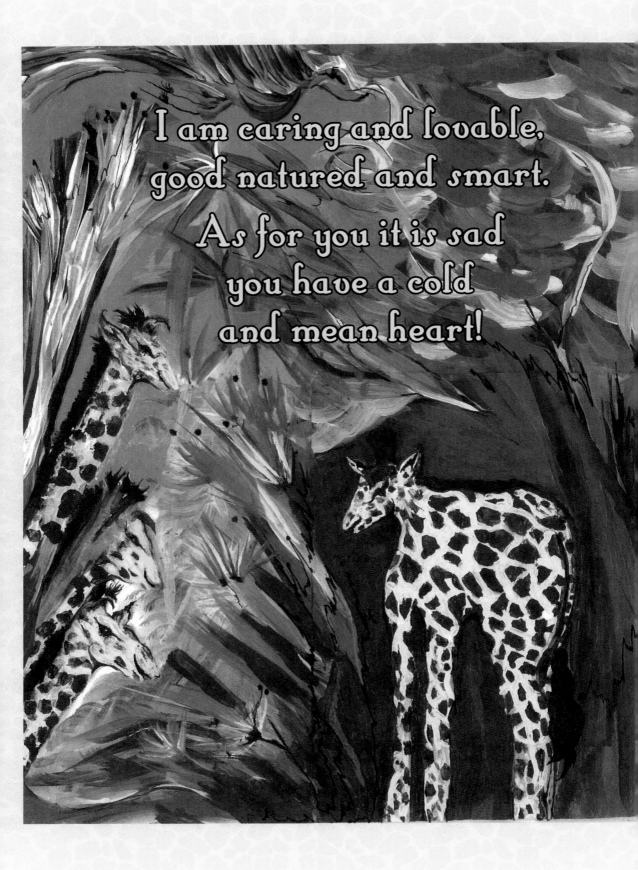

I am caring and lovable,
good natured and smart.
As for you it is sad
you have a cold
and mean heart!

It is never too late
to realize this,
to be kind to others,
it is compassion
you miss.

I have faith in you all
and I know you can be

giraffes as wondrous as your neck
for the entire world to see."

Now Little Laffe realized that
she was much worthy:

she was short-necked but quite cute
and pleasantly curvy.

Hence, she now made it known
she would have a good time

like the other giraffes
eating fig leaves
and guzzling sodas of lime.

She danced the night away
to the coolest of tunes

played by the well-known
hippy forest group
"The Bashful Buffoons."

They now finally understood
and wanted Little Laffe around.

but suddenly she was missing
and nowhere to be found.

On a bright, sunny and
marvelous day,

a giraffe that loved her
came her way.

To the other giraffes
it was no longer a surprise

that Little Laffe was beautiful
in his adoring eyes.

~~LOVE ALWAYS~~

SOME INTERESTING FACTS ABOUT GIRAFFES.

Giraffes are the tallest animals in the world.

These gentle giants are herbivores, which means they only eat plants.

Their very specialized stomachs have four chambers to digest food.

They are mostly found in the African savannas, grasslands, and woodlands.

Giraffes have only seven vertebrae in their very long necks, which is the same as most mammals.

Their excellent eyesight allows them to see hungry predators from far away.

They are very social animals and roam around in groups.

In the wild, these wonderful creatures can live for twenty five years. In captivity, they have been known to live for forty years.

The giraffe population is declining rapidly, and there are conservation groups to save them and other endangered species.

Made in the USA
Middletown, DE
11 October 2020